The House Whisperer

The House Whisperer

Becoming a Successful Home Inspector

GLENN STEWART

Copyright © 2015 Glenn Stewart

All rights reserved.

This book or any portion thereof
may not be reproduced or used in any manner whatsoever
without the express written permission of the publisher
except for the use of brief quotations in a book review.
Printed in the United States of America

First Printing, 2015

ISBN-13: 9781517664695
ISBN-10: 1517664691

Acknowledgements

After losing a Silicon Valley job during the dot.com bubble, it turned out not to be the end of the world. It was my realtor friend John Carter, who suggested I look into home inspections as a second career.

Rolland Pruner, a retired building contractor and home inspector, became my mentor, go-to guy and the person who suggested The House Whisperer business name.

My wife Patty Robins was by my side providing encouragement and motivation to get the book published and was overheard saying, "Hooray, it's finally done."

When I thought spell-check was enuff, Cindy Stewart, a retired teacher, reviewed my grammar and found much to my chagrin a myriad of edits.

I also want to recognize all the home owners whose homes I inspected, who made my day when I was telling myself "just when I think I've seen it all".

Table of Contents

	In The Beginning	xiii
Chapter 1	Is This For Me	1
Chapter 2	Ready, Set, Go	8
Chapter 3	Certified, Licensed, Insured	13
Chapter 4	Tools & Equipment	16
Chapter 5	Capture What You See	22
Chapter 6	Business Roadmap	25
Chapter 7	Getting the Word Out	29
Chapter 8	Phone Power	38
Chapter 9	Inspection Office	41
Chapter 10	Good Morning	43
Chapter 11	Inspection Fees	46
Chapter 12	Please Sign Here	50
Chapter 13	Stepping on Stage	53
Chapter 14	The Report	64
Chapter 15	Writing Right	67
Chapter 16	Super Service	70
Chapter 17	Within Reach	73
Chapter 18	Standards of Practice	77
Chapter 19	Code of Ethics for Home Inspectors	93

Introduction

The journey of a thousand miles begins with one step.
— Lao Tzu

It was during a job search, that a friend asked if I had considered inspecting houses as a living. The thought intrigued me.

What could be easier than looking at the condition of a house for a buyer, sending them a report and pocketing $295, $525, $750 or more?

If a condo a day was inspected for $265 that would be $1325 a week. Wow. Inspecting 5 houses a week at $395 each for 48 weeks and vacationing in Maui for 4 weeks would net $94,800 a year. I could do that. Think about the potential income by inspecting more than five properties a week.

With no prior training or experience in the building construction industry, I began exploring a career in home inspection as a business opportunity.

It came down to being in control of my life, being my own boss, the freedom to work my own hours, having a flexible work schedule, and making enough money to be comfortable.

Home inspecting isn't a get rich quick scheme, but a career that can develop over time. It isn't an easy path and certainly not for everyone.

If you're a motivated, detail-oriented person with good communication skills and are willing to roll-up your shirt sleeves; you'll find the home inspection business an extremely interesting and rewarding career.

Glenn Stewart, The House Whisperer

There are secrets to be revealed in this house on Main street.
- The House Whisperer

In The Beginning

Home Inspections

THE FIRST KNOWN home inspection company was, Home Equity Loss Protection Services (Glen Ellyn, IL), originally founded by Christopher P. Nolan and Loyola Professor Mark Goodfriend. The company was officially incorporated in the early 1980s. The history of home inspections can be found online at <u>Wikipedia Home Inspections</u>.

Today, real estate home inspections have become a standard practice in the home-purchasing process. A home inspection is a visual inspection of a residential structure and the components of a building to identify things that aren't functioning properly; pose a health and safety concern and/or need to be repaired or replaced.

The inspection provides an unbiased and objective opinion about the condition of residential properties: apartments, condominiums, townhouses, single family houses, multiplexes, etc. Home inspection is a career that requires a keen eye, knowledge about how a house is constructed, how it functions and continuous education for the inspector. It should be noted that a home inspection is not technically exhaustive and doesn't imply that every minor defect will be identified. Although home inspectors look for and report violations of local building codes, they aren't city code inspectors they're generalists.

People spend a lot of money to purchase a property and their expectations are high, but the bottom line is that no one likes surprises. Home buyers don't want to move into their new home and discover repairs, they weren't told about before signing on the dotted line. This is where competent home inspectors help home buyers and sellers make informed decisions about their pending real estate purchase.

Experienced home inspectors can earn between $250 to $1300+ a day examining the interiors and exteriors of residential buildings by observing property conditions and then describing those conditions in a written report. Inspectors are most often hired by prospective home buyers to examine the visible and readily accessible areas of a house. This includes the exterior and interior, kitchen, bathroom(s), foundation, roof, electrical, plumbing, heating and/or cooling system, attic, crawlspace, drainage, basements and the list goes on.

Today's savvy home inspector uses a smart phone, laptop-computer and/or tablet, voice recorder, camera, a few basic hand tools and may take field notes to conduct a home inspection. There are inspectors who use additional tools and detecting equipment to create comprehensive inspection reports; however, the use of advanced tools and equipment becomes a business decision those inspectors make.

It takes time to build your reputation and an inspection referral database. Inspection jobs most often originate from home inspectors who market themselves to home buyers, sellers, real estate agents, friends, the barber and just about anyone. There was a real estate downturn in 2008 that preceded the Great Recession. Since then, the demand for housing has continued to grow. Home sales have steadily increased along with the number of homes inspected; confirming that the home inspection business is once again in high demand.

Origins

In the beginning, some home buyers would move into a house and discover that there was no hot water; or that the house foundation had settled and cracked. This would prompt a phone call to their real estate agent, where the buyer complained, asked for repairs and/or threaten a lawsuit, if something wasn't done to correct the situation. Realtors and their brokers found themselves being responsible for not disclosing defects in the houses they were selling and paying for costly repairs. Home inspections evolved in the mid-1980s from realtors wanting to avoid liability and litigation after a house was sold to a buyer.

A landmark California court case occurred in 1984 (Easton vs. Strassburger) about a home seller failing to disclose known problems about his property to a home buyer. As a result, California Senate Bill 1406 was signed into law and mandated real estate disclosure. The law also required that real estate agents perform their own "diligent visual inspection" and disclose any defect that they might find.

Home buyers began to demand more information about the property they wanted to buy. This ranged from listing known repairs, remodeling or upgrading a house without building permits to conditions needing attention. Real estate disclosure laws now require home sellers to inform home buyers what they know about the property being sold. The California Association of Realtors altered their contract forms to include a provision for the home buyer to hire their own professional inspector. Hence the home inspection business emerged on the West Coast as an industry. Since then, one state after another adopted their own versions of California's disclosure laws leading to the emergence and expansion of the Home Inspection Industry.

Early home inspectors were mostly people who worked in the home building industry; and had a working knowledge of how a house was constructed and about defects that caused problems. They began inspecting houses issuing verbal and written reports. As home inspections evolved, the inspections themselves became standardized.

Standardization led to the creation of the American Society of Home Inspectors group (ASHI) in 1976. The California Real Estate Inspection Association (CREIA) in 1976... National Association of Home Inspectors (NAHI) in 1987... National Association of Certified Home Inspectors (NACHI) in 1990... and other inspection organizations followed.

These early organizations developed Standards of Practice and Code of Ethics. Standards of Practice define minimum requirements for what components or systems must be observed and reported during a home inspection. Examples of the Standards of Practice can be viewed at the inspection organizations listed above.

Code of Ethics are the guidelines which set out acceptable behaviors for home inspectors typically in the areas of honesty, objectivity and integrity. Many organizations govern themselves with such a code. This document usually starts with a section that states the purpose and goals of the parent inspection organization, and is followed by a section that sets the specific behavior standards for home inspectors.

Certified or licensed home inspectors belonging to an organized inspection group are most often sought after by home buyers and sellers, as there's assurance that the inspected real estate property will be thoroughly reviewed and a comprehensive report issued.

Today's home buyer is more sophisticated and demanding. They want to know all they can about their future home before making their final decisions. It's estimated that approximately 85 percent of the homes sold today in the United States are inspected prior to purchase. This means that the real estate market is still under-served and that the home inspection industry continues to demonstrate strong growth. There continues to be a steady increase in overall volume of home sales and the percentage of homes inspected.

This trend leaves plenty of room for many motivated people to become a home inspector and build a home inspection career, or launch a home inspection company. The initial investment dollars and the operating overhead needed to run a home inspection business are small compared to other businesses, making this a potential lucrative small business opportunity.

1

Is This For Me

According to the Occupational Outlook Handbook, 2012 - 2013 Edition... *"Employment of construction and building inspectors is expected to grow 12 percent over the 2012-2022 decade, about as fast as the average for all occupations. The routine practice of obtaining home inspections is a relatively recent development, causing employment of home inspectors to increase rapidly.*

The concern for public safety and a desire to improve the quality of construction should continue to increase demand for inspectors. Although employment of home inspectors should continue to grow, some states are increasingly limiting entry into the field to those with related work experience or to those who are certified or licensed."

Home inspection is closely related to the real estate industry, and as such, follows the seasonal variances inherent in the business of real estate sales. There will always be peaks and valleys in the real estate cycle. The good news is that the majority of home buyers want to understand the condition of the houses they're buying and they will hire home inspectors.

The human population continues to grow and people have to live somewhere, and as long as there's a demand for housing, there'll be a demand for good home inspectors. The future for home inspectors is very bright, as the real estate market continues to march on.

What It Takes

With any job search, you want to take a hard look into what the job requirements are before taking the plunge. Self assessment of your skills and traits is one of the keys to becoming a successful home inspector. Are you:

- Detail-oriented
- Able to recall
- Mechanically inclined
- A problem solver
- A self-starter
- Motivated
- A communicator
- A people person
- Dependable
- Reliable
- Entrepreneurial

<u>Detail-oriented</u> – These people pay attention and notice the little things. Nothing should escape your attention. It's your job to notice everything – and put it into a report.

<u>Able to recall</u> – Building codes and requirements continue to change and evolve. A particular aspect of construction may have been acceptable in years past, but has changed to improve health

and safety requirements. Being able to recall previous construction requirements is a big plus for an accurate home inspection report.

<u>Mechanically inclined</u> – Having a basic idea how things function and work from roof installations to plumbing configurations. This is where you commit yourself to continuous education.

<u>Problem solver</u> – Each and every home inspection presents itself like a puzzle and you need to figure out the bigger picture. Whether you're attempting to understand the source of a water stain on the ceiling or hear strange noises coming from the plumbing pipes, your ability to problem solve in your head will help in communicating to the home buyer what's going on with the condition in a house.

<u>Self-starter</u> – A person who has initiative and will do whatever it takes to be successful. It takes being a self-starter to launch your own home inspection business.

<u>Motivated</u> – Motivation is "what drives you" to take a particular action. The path to becoming a home inspector is not an easy one. Motivation is essential to be successful.

<u>Communicator</u> – You need strong verbal and written communication skills to be an effective home inspector. This starts with the initial meeting when you invite the buyer to participate in the home inspection process. You should be forthcoming and informative as you explain what you see during an inspection. Inspectors need to be able to create a concise and accurate home inspection report in a clear manner.

People person – Are you someone who enjoys being with other people rather than alone? As a home inspector, you're dealing with different personalities at every inspection and have to adapt with everyone you meet.

Dependable, Reliable – Can you be counted on to show up to the inspection on time; conduct a comprehensive inspection; write a detailed report and deliver it within 24 hours? The home buyers and/or the referring real estate agents are counting on you to present an accurate condition of an inspected property.

Entrepreneurial – Do you have the drive and feel comfortable organizing and managing a business in order to make money? Do you have what it takes to get you through the hard times? Do you have a competitive spirit? As in all businesses, it seems to be a battle with the competition to win market share - i.e., more home inspections.

If you answered 'yes' to these traits or feel you can work towards improving your skills and traits - a home inspection career may be for you.

Education

A home inspector is a generalist. There is no other line of work that prepares you to become a home inspector. Educating yourself about the various house systems is a must. A few systems found in a house include:

- Heating and cooling
- Electrical and plumbing
- Roof and foundation
- Windows, doors, wall and floor systems

Having knowledge of systems and components that are obsolete yet still in service, such as asbestos products, vermiculite attic insulation, Knob & Tube electrical wiring is necessary to understand in order to inspect older houses. Although construction related fields require an understanding of how homes are built, they almost never deal with the extended use and age related deterioration of components that the home inspector encounters daily.

If you have no background in construction work, don't work in a building trade or haven't done handyman jobs, your chances of succeeding in the home inspection field are diminished, but you're definitely not out.

Adopting a 'Can Do' attitude and learning through home inspection classroom training courses, online training courses, seminars, monthly inspector meetings, tag-along inspections, mentors, and field inspection experience should prove to be highly beneficial.

If there are doubts about what's involved in the home inspection service business, find a local home inspector to tag along with and observe what the inspector does. Ask questions. This is important because during a home inspection, it requires using a ladder, climbing roofs, looking in attics, crawling through dark crawlspaces, all in the name of locating cracks, leaks, water stains, health and safety concern, etc.

Challenges

Performing a home inspection looks easy. You walk into a house and identify conditions needing attention, document what you see, prepare a report and send it to the client. What could be easier than that?

The reality is that it isn't easy becoming a home inspector. The real estate inspection business is a challenging profession. It takes working capital (money), education, training, computer know-how, and possessing written and verbal skills to start an inspection career.

Whether you start as a one-man show, work for an established inspection company or buy an inspection franchise; you need to have the financial strength to support yourself while training to become a home inspector. Not only do you need to keep a roof over your head, put food on the table and pay the bills, there needs to be money for membership dues, marketing collateral (business cards, flyers, and brochures), errors and omissions insurance, a computer, smart phone, report writing software, inspections tools and a vehicle.

If you plan to start out as one-man show, count on a cash cushion to live on for at least the first six months minimum, because you won't likely have much of an income from home inspections. Conserve your money before you start. The first year is tough, and it's not easy to get inspections. As you become established as a known inspector, you can make $50,000 to $175,000+ every year.

Expect first year minimum startup costs to range from $4-6K for a computer, software, printer, phones, small office setup, inspection equipment, and E&O insurance; $500-$4000 for inspection training and memberships with professional organizations; $500 for business cards, brochures, flyers and other marketing collateral.

An alternate option is to start out working for an established home inspection company. Find out what they offer in terms of inspection training, equipment, transportation, employee benefits and what your out-of-pocket expenses would be. As a company employee, you take home a percentage of the inspection fee and are paid weekly.

New Inspectors

Newbie inspectors face a wall of challenges with minimal work experience, limited financial resources, fledgling credit histories and little to no inspection experience. They often have difficulty convincing people to schedule an inspection or convincing home inspection companies that they should be hired. The job requires a combination of formal training and hands-on experience to be able to identify what needs repair or review by a licensed contractor. In this day and age, home inspectors cannot afford to 'overlook' a property condition that needs attention. Minor oversights may occur, but failing to note big tickets items may be a trip before a judge.

Being computer savvy helps the inspector schedule inspections, confirm appointments and use report-writing programs. Reports are emailed to the client or hardcopy reports may be printed and delivered. Using the computer for word-processing and editing report comments is part of an inspector's job. Inspection comments are constantly being modified or revised to fit a particular property inspection.

Climbing a ladder to the roof, inspecting hillside properties, accessing the attic or crawling on your belly in a crawlspace can expose the inspector to personal safety and health risks, i.e. slipping, tripping, and breathing contaminated dust. There are other physical risks associated with inspecting such as falling off a ladder, climbing stairs, falling through the attic 'floor', and twisting an ankle. Proper training and staying physically fit are important to reduce these risks.

The successful home inspector possesses a combination of interpersonal, technical, managerial and communication/marketing skills. If you feel that you're made of the right stuff, are willing to work hard and want a new career — then read on.

2

Ready, Set, Go

Membership

THE HOME INSPECTOR wears many hats from being a detailed observer and house detective to being a report writer and a communication specialist. One of the biggest challenges of an enterprising I-want-to-be-a-home-inspector is the credibility gap. Your credibility in the eyes of buyers, sellers and real estate agents starts with being certified or licensed and experienced.

Whether you live in a state that requires licensing or in one that doesn't, you should become a member of a national or state recognized inspection organization. Go to Google and type the name of the state where you live along with "home inspection organizations". There are nationally recognized home inspection organization such as ASHI, NAHI, InterNACHI, AAHI, SPREI and various other state home inspections organizations such as in California (CREIA), Florida (FABI) or in Georgia (GAHI). Not all states have real estate inspection organizations at the state level.

Choose an inspection organization that follows both a Code of Ethics and Standards of Practice. Find out about annual dues and where chapter meetings are held. Most organization chapters hold monthly educational meetings and special event programs. Go to the organization's chapter meetings. Chapter meetings are an excellent way to meet and interact with other inspectors, participate in hands-on programs, learn about educational seminars and conferences, and to become familiar with the inspection industry.

Many inspection chapters have mentoring programs or ride-along programs, where people go with an experienced inspector to see what's involved during a field inspection. Chapter members can count on getting their questions answered. Once you are a member of an inspection organization, your education begins and will not stop, unless you opt out. Home inspectors in many states are required to take continuing education classes before renewing their licenses or memberships in home inspection associations.

Training

Many budding home inspectors make a mistake of starting out with little or no inspection training and this could eventually be their downfall. Training is the single most important step before engaging in your first home inspection.

Successful home inspectors have made a commitment to learn all they can about the inspection business. If the state where you will be operating requires a license, they will also likely require training. If the state where you will be operating does not require training, it's to your benefit to be fully prepared when performing inspections.

There are accredited and nationally recognized home inspection training schools that teach the advanced information that inspectors need to know to prepare for state and national exams or to fulfill continuing education requirements. Schools can help you start your own successful inspection business, be hired by an established home inspection company or provide a running start when buying a franchise.

There are also online training programs to learn about home inspection. Earning a home inspector certification online has its advantages and disadvantages.

An advantage, especially if you are a construction worker, contractor or work in the trades closely related to the field of home inspection, is that you learn about becoming a home inspector from home without having to attend a vocational school, since you're already familiar with house construction. In this case, an online program offers the flexibility and freedom that would be beneficial for working-trades people looking to get into home inspection.

A disadvantage of online training is that it doesn't provide the hands-on training and mentorship training that could be beneficial in becoming a home inspector, especially for those people who don't have a background in the trades.

The training institutes below offer classroom time, online or distance courses, and/or hands-on training:

- Kaplan Real Estate and Home Inspection Training
- American Home Inspector Training Institute
- Professional Home Inspection Institute
- Allied Home Inspection School

Most home inspection training companies offer flexible terms and financial assistance which makes training affordable.

Franchise

Getting into a home inspection franchise provides home inspectors a structured way to begin and grow their business. Franchise owners are able to run their home inspection business under the franchise's brand name, and receive training, marketing and business operations support. Be sure that you fully investigate a franchise before signing a contract. Check out the pros and cons of buying a franchise (Google: Nolo franchise pros cons). Buying into a home inspection franchise often requires $25,000 to $60,000 working capital. Research the various home inspection franchise opportunities online.

Mentors

With training under your belt - having a mentor is a great way to help you learn more about getting started as a home inspector, especially if you're wondering how to start inspecting. A mentor is that one person who takes you under their wing and nurtures your career quest. A mentor is someone who you can ask questions of and who can guide, listen and advise you.

There is no substitute for field experience as a budding home inspector. No amount of schooling can compare to the real life experience and training you can receive with an experienced home inspector who is willing to mentor you. Finding an experienced home inspector at your local chapter meeting should prove to be an easy task. Many seasoned inspectors enjoy sharing their knowledge with you and help you avoid some of the mistakes they made earlier in their career. From a mentor's perspective, the benefit they get is the satisfaction of helping you out and knowing that they are someone whose opinion you hold in high regard.

Reference Books

Don't make the mistake by starting out under-educated. Building a personal home inspection reference library can be an invaluable source of education and reference. There are books, CDs, videos, courses, seminars and other materials which provide home inspectors with information on building codes, home construction, electrical systems, plumbing systems, heating and cooling systems, roofs, fireplaces and chimneys, and the list goes on. Education resources are widely available, but vary widely in quality and content. Seek out the advice and recommendations of other home inspectors and from home inspection organizations.

Inspection of residential property is based on building codes. Building codes exist to protect the public's health, safety and welfare. There are code reference books for the International Residential Code (IRC), Uniform Plumbing Code (UPC), National Electrical Code (NEC), International Code Council (ICC) and many, many more.

Buying all these code books can be expensive, and reading code books is a daunting task that makes for some dry reading. Most libraries have building code reference books you can browse through. Learning how to navigate through these building code books is a worthwhile exercise.

Some years ago, a former electrician and building inspector for the city of Oakland, CA teamed up with a general contractor and a certified combination inspector to extract the meaningful content from the code books and compiled the information into today's popular series of Code Check books.

Code Check books are condensed guides of the building, electrical, plumbing, and HVAC codes and can be found online (www.codecheck.com) and in bookstores. This series of books is recommended for home inspectors to help educate themselves about the inspection business. Being familiar with the codes is essential for a successful home inspector.

3

Certified, Licensed, Insured

Certified, Licensed or Not

As of this printing, there are 39 states that have regulations affecting home inspectors. Many states require a license or certification for employment as a real estate home inspector. Check with your state licensing board to see if home inspectors are required to be licensed in your state. Some states including Alabama, Pennsylvania, and Maryland require membership or approval by a national home inspector association as a condition for licensing.

Your chances of being selected by a buyer or realtor as their inspector of choice are much greater if you're certified or licensed as a home inspector in your state, carry errors and omissions insurance, follow a code of ethics and standards of practice, and continually educate yourself.

American Home Inspectors Training institute provides a US map of state regulations (Google: AHIT States) and click on your State. Whether you become licensed or certified, you'll be viewed as an inspector with credentials that will help you stand out from the crowd.

In other states where home inspectors aren't regulated, anyone with a business card, an official-looking checklist and a flashlight can set up shop as a home inspector with little or no training or classroom time. If something of significance is missed during one of their inspections (live electrical wires in the family room or a cracked foundation), there's a good chance that a lawsuit is headed their way.

E&O and Liability Insurance

Errors and omissions insurance or E&O is the insurance that covers you individually in the event that a home buyer or seller holds you responsible for a home inspection, where an error or omission on your part caused a financial loss for them. The insurance covers you for errors (or omissions) that you made or that the client perceives you made. Most E&O policies cover judgments, settlements and defense costs. Even if the allegations are found to be groundless, thousands of dollars may be needed to defend the lawsuit. A lawsuit can put a home inspection company out of business.

Why should a home inspector have insurance coverage? Simply put, everyone makes mistakes. Nobody is perfect. It would be a sad day to lose everything that you did to become a home inspector, if you didn't carry errors and omissions insurance. Most E&O insurance policies come with personal liability coverage to protect inspectors. As a home inspector, you have two exposures that are covered by personal liability insurance that typically accompanies E&O insurance:

<u>Property Damage</u> - You missed calling out a broken water supply pipe and the house is damaged; a ladder slips and damages a car parked on the driveway, or the inspector accidentally knocks over a priceless Ming vase.

Bodily Injury – You didn't report that the basement stairs handrail was missing and the service repairman falls down the steps suffering injury. Bodily injury exposure is the one with the greatest potential for large claim settlements.

Actuarial data shows that new inspectors are more likely to get a claim during their first 12 months of business. It's for this reason that many insurance carriers refuse to underwrite home inspectors who are new to the profession, or if they do, the home inspector's insurance premiums are quite high. There are insurance carriers who have a pay-per-inspection program to help new inspectors get started or for inspectors who only do a few inspections per year.

There are insurance companies that welcome new inspectors to the home inspection industry like OREP, FREA, and Allen Insurance. Their insurance programs are available in all 50 states. As long as applicants can show evidence of formal training from an approved school, they can insure you. Google: home inspector E&O (your State)

An inspection business with errors and omissions insurance will only pay the policy deductible, which may be the difference between spending a couple thousand dollars or losing your business.

4

Tools & Equipment

Inspector Tools

A FEW BASIC HAND tools, such as, an electrical tester, screwdrivers, a flashlight and ladder are enough to get you started inspecting houses. As you get more inspections under your belt, you may find yourself adding additional tools and equipment. Home inspector tools can be found at local hardware, retail and specialty stores.

The tools and equipment listed below have been used successfully by the author. Group 1 tools are carried in a tool pouch; Group 2 gear is used in the crawlspace; and Group 3 tools/equipment are found in the vehicle and used occasionally.

Group 1 - Tool Pouch

The basic tools for inspection can be carried in a small leather 2-4 pocket tool pouch worn around the waist or in a tool vest. These tools include a flashlight, camera, screwdrivers, small tape measure, electrical tester, infrared thermometer, ID dots, and slip-on booties

The first Eveready <u>flashlight</u> patent was issued in 1898 and produced a 'flash' of light. Today, LED flashlight technology produces a very white and bright light beam, perfect for home inspectors. Consider rechargeable flashlights, otherwise, you'll be spending a lot of money on batteries. Most inspectors carry two flashlights - one that's charging and one that's being used during the inspection.

Using a digital <u>camera</u> to take photos of conditions during a home inspection helps document what was observed and allows the homebuyer to visually see what needs attention. Sometimes a photo is worth a thousand words. Inspection report photos have protected many a home inspector involved in litigation. Using a camera puts you ahead of the competition, particularly the inspectors who don't use a camera.

Consider buying a ruggedized camera with a rechargeable battery, a 2x-4x lens zoom and an extra battery. The new cameras are waterproof, shockproof, coldproof, and dust/sand proof. They are tough enough to survive the crawlspace and the occasional drop.

Other Tools
Carry a couple of <u>screwdrivers</u> in the tool pouch for removing heating furnace covers, electrical panel covers, prying open stuck covers, poking wood support post bases, etc. A flat blade screwdriver (5/16" x 8") and #2 Phillips usually gets the job done.

Use a small <u>tape measure</u> to determine required spacing and height requirements of stair steps, window openings, handrail/guardrail height and spacing. More accidents and lawsuits occur due to improper stair and railing construction.

Buy an inexpensive electrical wall <u>receptacle tester</u> to verify that a wall outlet is wired properly. Plug it into an outlet and observe the state of the lights. A small label (legend) on the tester identifies what the configuration of lights means.

Identification dots help people locate what part of a door is rubbing, which wall outlet in the bedroom is not working or which window in the living room doesn t latch. Use something like Avery #5790 ¼" diameter red dots●. It's a good visual. And don't forget to mention 'red dot' in the inspection report: *"One of the electrical wall outlets in the right side bedroom is damaged and marked with a red dot."*

At many inspections, there may be a "Remove Your Shoes" sign, as the homeowner doesn't want their snow white carpet dirtied by the bottom of people's shoes. Carry slip-on shoe covers and use them as a courtesy.

Use a handheld, non-contact infrared thermometer to measure surface temperatures at electrical panels, circuit breakers, heating/cooling registers, and water stream temperature without contact. Just aim, pull the trigger and read the surface temperature in less than a second. An infrared thermometer can help identify potential problems.

Group 2 – Crawlspace Gear

Crawlspaces can be dusty, dirty and muddy and just down right unsafe. Inspectors want to protect themselves from the contaminants such as fiberglass, mold spores, rodent droppings that can be stirred up when inspecting. It's recommended purchasing protective clothing, such as overalls, gloves, knee and elbow pads, and a high quality respirator to avoid breathing in crawlspace dust.

Start with coveralls. You can buy permanent coveralls which are washable, or disposable coveralls that are thrown out after 10-15 'crawls'. Some disposable coveralls are made from Tyvek, a synthetic material that is strong and hard to tear. It's a trade-off in terms of the difference in the cost between the two types of coveralls, as you wash the permanent coveralls and end up using water and electricity/gas. There are also disposable coveralls with attached booties and a hood.

<u>Gloves</u> protect your hands as you move around in a crawlspace. There always seems to be dust, dirt, rodent carcasses, broken glass, nails, abandoned items to be moved, spider webs, etc. that your hands are coming into contact with.

In most crawlspaces, the clearance is limited and you literally crawl on your belly or move around on your hands and knees. Investing in <u>knee pads</u> and forearm/<u>elbow pads</u> will save your knees and elbows from bruising and puncture wounds, and give your coveralls more service life. To protect your forearms, consider buying 18" or longer welders gloves that cover your forearms, or buy a pair of kids' soccer shin guards. The shin guards have a hard plastic shield and easily pull onto your forearms.

In crawlspaces, there is one piece of equipment which is highly recommended - a <u>dust respirator</u>. A respirator is designed to protect your lungs from breathing in dirt dust, contaminated dust where rodents have been, pollens, mold spores, fiberglass and other contaminants. The cloth mouth mask works to some degree, but they don't effectively seal around your nose and mouth. Invest in a high quality air respirator; you'll be glad you did.

Group 3 – Vehicle Stored Items
Not all house roofs can or should be walked on, due to the type of roofing material, the height, the roof slope or if it has rained. Here's where a pair of <u>binoculars</u> can provide a limited inspection of the roof. A good binocular choice for inspecting roofs, flashing material and chimneys are 7x35, 8x40, or 10x50 binoculars.

The 7, 8, 10 numbers are the amount of magnification, i.e. 7x, 8x or 10x times closer. If you can't walk on a roof, be sure to recommend a roof inspection by a licensed roofer in your report prior to the close of the contingency period as there may be reportable conditions.

A <u>ladder</u> is necessary for home inspections. A straight, folding, or telescoping ladder that extends to 16 feet should be sufficient for inspections. Telescoping ladders collapse to 24" long, weigh less than 25 lbs and will fit in a sports car. If a longer ladder is needed for roof access, it's recommended that a review of the roof be scheduled with a licensed roofing contractor, unless you want to carry a 27 foot extension ladder.

Some inspectors have a toolbox with backup tools, such as a hammer, pry bar, pliers, small drill, utility knife, awl, a 1" diameter steel ball bearing to see if there's any floor slope, and a main water shutoff T-bar.

The <u>utility knife</u> can help cut the caulking seal on attic access panels or a paint seal around electrical subpanels, so that there's a clean cut on the paint seal.

Use an <u>awl</u> to help pull back a carpet at a floor corner. Sometimes you want to inspect the floor underneath a carpet to check for water damage, especially under windows and in bathrooms where carpet has been installed.

Roll a large diameter steel <u>ball bearing</u> (1-2" diameter) on solid surface floors to see if there's any appreciable floor slope, a possible indicator of foundation settlement or poor construction.

Specialty Equipment

There are specialty tool stores that cater to experienced home inspectors, offering sophisticated equipment such as moisture meters, infrared cameras, gas detectors, etc. Although not required by Standards of Practice, some inspectors feel that this equipment allows them to provide a more valuable and in-depth inspection, giving them an advantage over the competition.

It's The House Whisperer's opinion that a home inspector using specialized tools and equipment does not make the user an expert, unless you've had previous experience with specialized tools or have been certified in their use. For example, in a court of law, a home inspector who used a moisture meter to identify a moisture problem in the basement, but missed the wet wall in a bathroom will lose his case. The choice as to what tools and equipment a home inspector will use on the job is a business decision each inspector makes.

First Impressions

Do looks matter at the inspection site? In a word, yes. How the home buyer and agent see you has a direct relationship on your referrals. Your attire, grooming, business card, brochure, car, etc. all play a big part in those first 90 seconds when you meet at the inspection site.

Clothing is the primary focus in creating a positive first impression with people. It increases your perceived status with clients and agents, and it helps with your confidence. Jeans, a t-shirt and sneakers may be the casual dress in your town, but a pair of Dockers, a logoed polo shirt and good work shoes signal to others a good first impression, that you are a professional. If a person isn't dressed for the occasion, people will notice their clothing; but if you're dressed for the inspection, they will notice the person.

For the home inspector, it's about building trust, confidence and a mini relationship before you start the inspection. People will trust their eyes before they'll trust your words.

5

Capture What You See

Inspection Data

IN THE BEGINNING, home inspectors took paper and pen with them to take field notes and documented what they observed during an inspection. Back at their desk, they would type up a report and mail or hand deliver it.

The time consuming field notes evolved into a checklist form, where the inspector would put a checkmark or an 'X' in a box next to a comment on the form, and added a few additional written words to clarify conditions. But this method didn't convey what might happen if the condition wasn't corrected or stipulate recommended action by others. This exposed the inspector to possible litigation.

With the advent of the digital age - desktop computers, laptops, and pocket PCs, inspection reporting software was developed with templates, checklists and comment libraries. The new technology allowed the home inspector to enter their findings into their hardware devices by typing or tapping with a stylus. Additional field notes were recorded on a separate voice recorder or written down and home inspectors would still spend more hours back at their desk adding notes and editing their reports.

When camera film evolved into digital images, inspectors began to use digital cameras to document conditions in need of attention during their inspections. The digital photos could be easily be inserted into the inspection report saving considerable time matching photos to inspection comments. Home buyers and their real estate agents were now able to see what the inspector saw especially in attics and crawlspaces.

Today, the touch-screen computer tablet and smartphone, which are small, light-weight technological marvels for the home inspector, can be set up with improved report-writing software created for this technology. This allows the inspector to select an inspection comment on the device, take a photo which matches up with the selected comment, and record field notes in the palm of their hand. This technology has significantly reduced the amount of time to edit an inspection report; and allows the inspection report to be emailed to the client within 24 hours, so the homebuyer can make timely decisions.

Before choosing inspection reporting software, it's worth the time investment to request demonstration software from several inspection report writing companies and compare them in order to see which software is right for you. By asking other home inspectors what inspection software they use, you'll find differences in the features, including ease of navigation, price and customer support. Nearly all of the inspection software programs offer various templates to produce reports for residential, commercial, and multi-family units, as well as different forms and more.

These companies offer home inspection reporting software:

- Home Gauge
- Home Inspector Pro
- 3D Inspection Software

- Inspect IT
- Report Host
- Horizon by Carson Dunlop
- Spectacular
- EZ Home Inspection Software

6

Business Roadmap

Marketing Plan

MARKETING IS EVERYTHING an inspector does to get a home inspection scheduled. It's talking to realtors, neighbors, your dentist, stopping by open houses, handing out business cards, distributing flyers, creating a website, blogging, using social media sites, attending realtor marketing meetings, seminars, joining networking business groups, writing articles for a local newspaper, making presentations at realtor offices, and more. As you can see, there are a lot of things to do. Without a marketing plan, many home inspectors may feel overwhelmed.

A marketing plan is a document which outlines the ways to promote a business. A well-thought-out marketing plan can be used to develop and grow an inspection business. It helps inspectors focus on goals and keeps them on track. An effective home inspection marketing plan allows inspectors to control their destiny. It formalizes ideas, keeps you focused, and helps establish goals. It will help the inspector understand their clients, the competition and the real estate market environment so much better.

Planning is an absolute necessity if the inspector wants to be successful. Marketing plans vary in content, but should target a few key areas to create a road map for a new home inspection career. <u>Keep it simple</u> and write it down on one piece of paper answering these questions:

- Who and where is your target market?
- What is your business statement?
- What is your unique selling proposition?
- What goals do you want to set?

Target Market

Identify the counties and towns where you want to do inspections. Decide who you'll target for your marketing efforts: homeowners, real estate offices, realtor marketing meetings, open houses and/or top-producing agents.

Business Statement

The business statement is a brief description of a home inspector's fundamental purpose. What do you want to accomplish? Think about this question and write down a business statement.

Example: The purpose of the Best Home Inspections is to be the 'go to' residential inspection company in town by conducting thorough inspections generating comprehensive reports and providing outstanding customer service.

Unique Selling Proposition (USP)

Your unique selling proposition is when you can pinpoint what makes your inspection business unique from your competitors. A USP sets you apart from your competition, positioning your inspection company as the more logical choice among homebuyers and realtors. Create a list of things that sets your company apart from the competition: a same day report (the report within 24 hours), work on Saturday, available 7 days a week, inspect in multiple counties, no charge for out buildings, competitive pricing, and service with a smile.

Ask yourself this question about your inspection business to determine a USP: What is unique about your inspection business?

Examples:
InterNACHI: *"Inspected Once, Inspected Right"*
Best Home Inspections: *"One Call Does It All – Home, Termite, Roof"*
FedEx: *"Our most important package is yours"*
Campbell's Soup: *"Mmm! Mmm! Good!"*

Goal Setting

Goal Setting involves establishing specific, measurable, achievable, and realistic objectives. Why should you set goals? Earl Nightingale put it this way, *"People with goals succeed because they know where they are going. It's as simple as that."*

Here are four reasons to set goals as a home inspector:

- Sets up a target to aim for
- Focuses your time and effort

- Provides motivation, persistence and desire
- Creates a roadmap to take you from where you are to where you want to be

When setting your goals, make them clear and concise, meaningful and measurable, and consider approaching them from a grand scale. Goals can help you focus your time and energy. Here are a few ideas:

- 10 inspections a week
- Go to Open Houses on Saturday
- Visit 1 real estate office a day
- Join the Chamber of Commerce, go to their mixers

There are a few home inspection marketing companies that can help you with your marketing plan. One company that stands out is the The Savvy Inspector, who can help launch, grow and manage your new home inspection company. When you're ready, check them out: www.thesavvyinspector.com

7

Getting the Word Out

Customer Service

SERVICE IS THE main ingredient of the home buying experience. When inspectors provide outstanding customer service to their clients and their agents, they can expect a reward of repeat business from the realtors and referrals from home buyers. It's up to you, the home inspector to consistently provide outstanding service so they will come back with repeat business. The benefits and savings from not having to re-market to get new clients will be beneficial to the bottom line.

In the past, the inspection report would be available in a couple of days. No longer is this the case. Providing the report within 24 hours is the new norm. Sending the report to home buyers and realtors in a timely fashion is good customer service.

Another way to offer great customer service is to be flexible when scheduling inspections. Monday through Friday is when most inspectors schedule their inspections. Opening up your schedule to include Saturday availability or even an occasional Sunday to accommodate an emergency inspection goes a long ways to improving your image as an inspector who offers outstanding customer service.

The next best thing to having real estate agents give an inspector repeat business is to have them tell others about their experience and recommend your inspection company. At the end of the day, delivering on a promise and having an outstanding inspection service will take your business to the next level and make you a more successful home inspector.

Advertising is getting the word out about your home inspection company. For startup businesses, there usually isn't much available money to devote to advertising. With limited funds, home inspectors want to make sure that they are going to get the best return on every advertising dollar that they spend.

Yellow Pages vs Internet

There was a time when home inspection companies advertised in the printed Yellow Pages and mailed out a monthly newsletter. In the last 10 years, the Internet has become the dominant source of advertising. Two-thirds of people looking for local services turn to the Internet. It's critical that an inspection business is properly represented or they risk losing inspections to the next guy.

Let's take a look at the Yellow Pages (YP) verses Internet media:

Getting the word out about your company
- YP: good local distribution
- Internet: can reach many people

Who are you?
- YP: trusted source
- Internet: people research to learn about you

Letting people know about your company
- YP: published once a year
- Internet: quick start marketing, anytime

Cost to advertise my company
- YP: expensive advertising
- Internet: inexpensive advertising

Can people find my company?
- YP: ad is always in phone book
- Internet: unpredictable online traffic

While Yellow Pages and Internet advertising may at first appear to be somewhat balanced, there is a large plus for Internet advertising. This is because Internet advertising can be cumulative. As your Internet website spends more time online, and as you drive more traffic to it through your advertising, the search engines' trust in your site will grow, and the benefits of each online advertising campaign will slowly build upon each other. This snowball effect of advertising is not likely to be achieved through the more traditional Yellow Pages advertising.

Websites

A website is a collection of related web pages containing text, images, videos or other digital assets. You can use your website to advertise, market and blog (write articles, share photos) about your inspection company. Computer literate home inspectors may create their own website using any number of online companies that provide website design tools and easy to use website templates, while other inspectors who aren't tech-savvy can hire a web designer to create a custom website.

Website design is a tradeoff between time and money. To create a website, you need either time or money - or both. Time and money often substitute for each other. You can pay dollars to have a website up and running in 2-4 weeks. Or you can spend your time (save cash) building a website and have it up and running in 2-4 months or longer. There are affordable website design companies that specialize in creating home inspection websites, but their website designs can turn out to have more of a 'cookie-cutter' appearance that will not grab the attention of potential customers. It can be to your advantage to ensure that you have a website that stands out above the competition.

Websites need more than a good design and great content. A comprehensive advertising campaign is the only way to make a website successful. Not only do home inspectors have to tempt potential home buyers and sellers to hire them, but they also have to tempt them to schedule an inspection appointment. It's the benefits of using your inspection company that will hook your home buying client. And that 'hook' will have them calling for inspections. But if they don't know what the benefits are of using a home inspection company's inspection services, they'll be on a competitor's website faster than a speeding bullet.

Keep websites updated and give people a reason to come back. Post a newsletter or post testimonials from your customers. Testimonials prove your client satisfaction, as well as establish your credibility.

How many websites have you visited with grammatical errors or words misspelled? It looks unprofessional and makes would-be customers wonder about the professionalism of your company. Proofread your web page copy. A poorly written web page is worse than not having a web page at all. If writing isn't your thing, find someone who can help you with your web page content.

Social Media

Social media includes websites and applications that enable people to create and share content or to participate in social networking.

Facebook can be used as a highly effective business tool. It's great for marketing your inspection service and connecting with your clients. Home inspectors should create a business Facebook page as it's an extension of your business; and lets people know about your services.

Use Twitter to quickly share information with people interested in your inspection services. If your business is not part of this exchange, you're leaving opportunities untouched. Create a business Twitter account. Twitter can benefit an inspection business with increased networking and marketing opportunities.

Other sites that will give you exposure for your business include Google+, LinkedIn, and Pinterest.

Blogs

Blog is an abbreviated version of "web log," which is a term used to describe web sites that maintain an ongoing chronicle of information, i.e., all about home inspections, an article on roofs, photos, tips, etc.

A blog features diary-type commentary and links to articles on other Web sites. Blogs range from personal, to business and political, and can focus on a range of subjects or one narrow subject such as home inspection.

Blogging continues to gain in popularity, as the Internet becomes more social. By sharing inspection photos and talking about home inspections, your business gains more exposure resulting in more requested inspections.

Flyers

Marketing flyers can be circulated at real estate offices and are a great way to promote a home inspection company. It's an opportunity to talk with realtors about your inspection business. The trick is making sure a flyer captures the realtors' attention. The design of a flyer makes a big difference in generating attention, as does the paper that the flyer is printed on. Here are a few tips to make flyers stand out from the crowd.

1. Create a great headline or title to capture people's attention. Make it memorable.
2. Keep the layout simple. Include a generous amount of white space.
3. Print on colored paper with black text to minimize costs.
4. Use an unusual photo or a graphic to support the title.
5. Offer a $25 discount coupon.

Postcards

Postcards are another medium to use to get the word out to people. There are several online printers that provide templates for creating your own postcard or they can design one for you. A popular and affordable online printing company is Vistaprint.

Presentations

Real estate office presentations are a great way to get in front of real estate agents in order to 'sell' your company to them. Many times it's the real estate agent who will refer a home inspector to their clients, if they know who you are.

Most real estate offices have meetings where they discuss sales, listings, what the current real estate marketing is doing, etc., that keep the real estate agents up to date on the market in their area. Often the office manager will have a guest speaker or a presentation by a third-party service (your inspection company). It's an opportunity to earn some referral business from the real estate agents.

Talk about anything house-related. Keep the presentation short. Answer questions. Chances are good that realtors will call for a home inspection.

Press Release

Press Releases are like a ticket to publicity, one that can get your company coverage in publications or on TV and radio stations.

Write a press release about how you've just launched a home inspection company with unique features or benefits. The press release should provide useful information for the reader including the benefits of using your inspection company. The trick to writing a press release is providing newsworthy information for the reader. Find out what the other home inspection companies are doing in town, and then find a newsworthy angle, such as offering something different, or giving a good reason why people should call your company.

Referrals

In order to expand an inspection business, you need more inspections. A good way to get more inspections is to get more referrals. A great source of referrals for home inspectors is from home buyers, sellers and real estate agents.

Why referrals should be revered:

- There's a minimum amount of effort involved. When talking to a real estate agent ask, "Is there anyone in your office who can use our inspection services?"
- There's an element of trust in an inspector when a referred agent learns of Best Inspections from one of their peers. People will work with people they trust.
- Word-of-mouth referrals are viewed as free advertising. How else can an inspector advertise/market themselves for zero dollars?

Proven ways to increase referrals:

- When meeting a potential homebuyer and their agent, hand them each 2-3 of your business cards to give to their friends and colleagues.
- Be the best inspector possible during your inspections by going above and beyond the call of duty. Do courtesy handyman items in front of the real estate agent such as, tightening loose door knobs, installing missing electrical outlet protection covers, etc... you'll get more referrals.
- A great time to ask for referrals is after the home inspection. Most people like to help other people.
- Referrals should always be asked for in the presence of others. People are more likely to refer other people if you're standing in front of them.
- Build the referral process into your weekly inspections. For example, drop a Thank You card on the kitchen counter after finishing an inspection of an owner occupied house.

At the bottom of the card, offer $25 off an inspection, include an activation code, so if that homeowner orders an inspection, you know to discount their inspection fee.

Remember: However you get them - referrals are the best possible customers your home inspection business can have.

8

Phone Power

One Phone Call

IT TAKES ONE phone call to schedule an inspection. Are you ready? It's a fact that most real estate agents have more than one home inspector they refer to their clients. When they call to schedule an inspection and the phone isn't answered by the 3rd or 4th ring, there's a chance they'll call someone else, especially if they're in a hurry to schedule.

New home inspectors initially answer the phone themselves, as they're usually on a shoestring budget and can't afford to hire someone to answer the phone. For anyone calling to schedule an inspection, if the phone isn't picked up by the 3rd ring, you may lose an inspection and maybe a referring agent as well.

Research shows that each additional ring after three makes 10% of the callers more likely to hang up and 15% of them more likely to be irritated when the phone is answered. There will be times when it's not convenient to answer the phone - like when driving in heavy traffic, crawling in a crawlspace, at the top of a ladder, or in the middle of an inspection summary with the client and agent. If a call can't be taken right then, there's the risk of losing another inspection to the competition.

Remember, answering promptly within one to three rings conveys a strong nonverbal message that a home inspection business is more efficient and it improves the odds of scheduling more inspections.

Yes, the inspector can answer the business phone when there are only one or two inspections coming in per week. However, as the number of home inspection requests increase, there's a chance of losing business if the phone can't be answered in a timely fashion, because you're out an inspection or the answering machine picks up.

Telephone Voice

Did you know the way in which you answer the telephone can say a lot about you as a person? In fact, the way you answer the phone could make or break your new inspection company.

When you respond to a call on the telephone in a pleasant and professional demeanor, the caller is more endeared to you and will often respond positively. Because people cannot 'see' over the telephone, they will form an opinion based not only on what we say, but also on 'how' we say it. Thus, the message we communicate over the telephone is based on two qualities: <u>what</u> we say and <u>how</u> we say it.

Studies[*] have indicated that as much as 87% of the opinions people form about us when speaking to us on the phone are based on the tone of our voice. Only 13% is based on the actual words we use. We all do this. People can "hear" our personality and mannerisms through the tone of our voice.

---

[*] Your Telephone Speaking Voice by Lenny Laskowski

Do you have telephone answering skills? You may be thinking, well I'll set up a phone answering machine to take my inspection calls and get back to the caller at the end of the day. If you allow a telephone answering machine to take a message, the result is often less eager. Regardless of how friendly the telephone answering machine's voice may appear, the fact is that robots are cold and impersonal. You will lose inspections.

For small businesses to be truly successful, you need someone to answer the business phone and be your office. Setting up an office space is a business decision you'll have to make.

9

Inspection Office

IT'S EASY TO miss a phone call while in a crawl space, attic or talking to the client. No home inspector can afford to miss a call. If it happens a lot, you're going to lose inspections and income. This is the reason a majority of home inspectors have set up an office space for someone to answer the phone, or they have signed up with a home inspection call center.

Home Office

Start by setting up a work surface in a bedroom, a closet, in a room corner, hallway or on the kitchen island, and populate the 'office space' with the basics: computer, multi-function printer, phone, comfortable chair and good lighting. Congratulations, you now have an office.

The office must be able to:

- Answer the phone by the third ring
- Promote your inspection company
- Capture information for an inspection via phone, fax or email

- Quote inspection fees, offer discounts and answer general questions
- Send reports, invoices, and receipts
- Call third-party service companies (termite, chimney, etc.)
- Handle cancellations, re-scheduling requests

Call Center

A second option for establishing an office is to contact a professional answering service for home inspectors, where they answer the phone and handle your inspection calendar and scheduling. Inspection call centers can:

- Schedule, re-schedule, cancel inspections
- Provide price quotations
- Sell and book inspection appointments
- Answer questions and promote the inspector's services
- Handle non-appointment related calls

Market services such as thank-you calls and competitor research
Home inspection call centers to check out:

- America's Call Center
- Inspector Services Group
- Center of the Sun
- Home Inspector Call Center

Whatever way you decide to go, having an office allows you to spend more time focusing on becoming a great home inspector and growing your new home inspection business, and less time worrying about office issues and missed phone calls.

10

Good Morning

Inspection Work Order

BY NOW YOU'VE put a lot of time, effort and money into marketing and advertising your inspection business and the hard work begins to pay off as the phone is ringing 5 or 6 times a week. You're now faced with the task of educating yourself or your office about booking an inspection order.

It's Monday morning and the phone rings. You can't believe what you're hearing, when Ms Super Agent from one of the largest real estate offices in your area calls to schedule an inspection. Are you ready to book that inspection and put it on the calendar?

After answering the phone in your best telephone voice, *"Good morning, this is Heidi at Best Home Inspections. How may I assist you?"* you'll need an inspection scheduling form or a computer program to ensure that the pertinent information is captured when inspection calls come in.

A form is used to capture specific information about the house to be inspected. Knowing where the property is located, how far you have to drive, and the size and age of the house helps determine how much will be charged for the inspection. The scheduling form can be used as your inspection work order, which you can take with you on an inspection to know who's who, as well as information about the property and any notes.

An inspection form needs to capture sufficient information about the property to be inspected. The most common information captured to schedule an inspection includes:

DATE _____
INSPECTION ADDRESS _____
INSPECTION DATE _____
INSPECTION TIME ___
TYPE: SINGLE FAMILY   CONDO   TOWNHOUSE   DUPLEX
OCCUPIED or VACANT   YEAR BUILT _____ SIZE SQ FT _____
ROOF: 1 OR 2 STORY _____ UTILITIES: ON   OFF
FOUNDATION: CRAWLSPACE   SLAB   BASEMENT
INSPECTION FEE _____ CASH   CHECK   CREDIT CARD

CLIENT'S NAME _____
PHONE _____
EMAIL _____

BUYER'S AGENT _____
OFFICE _____ ADDRESS _____ OFFICE PHONE _____
EMAIL _____
CELL PHONE _____

SELLER'S AGENT _____
OFFICE _____ ADDRESS _____ OFFICE PHONE _____
EMAIL _____
CELL PHONE _____

NOTES:

Filing System

It's a good idea to have an inspection work order filing system for record keeping and to be able to reference a report readily when someone calls with a question regarding the inspection.

Setting up a filing cabinet with hanging folders (manual system) is a great way to start, but it'll eventually become cumbersome and inefficient in trying to maintain it. The problem with a manual filing system is finding an inspection work order at a later date after conducting hundreds of inspections.

Clients and real estate agents who call with questions about past home inspections usually refer to the street address where the inspection took place. *"You inspected my house at 123 Main St a year ago, and I have a question about..."*

Inspection work orders filed manually are likely to be filed by the date of the inspection, not the street address, which makes it difficult to locate the original inspection work order and report.

Setting up a filing system on the computer is the most efficient way to organize your inspections. Consider using an online home inspection software program, which can help you keep track of your home inspections, maintain your realtor and client database (very important), search for a specific address, and send out your reports. These programs fill in your online inspection calendar, can add an event (dentist appt) to the calendar and allow you to view any of your past or currently-scheduled inspections.

Here are online home inspection scheduling and calendar software programs to simplify your office:

- Inspection Support Network
- The Schedule Center
- HomeGauge

11

Inspection Fees

Inspection Fees

OFTEN HOME BUYERS and real estate agents ask, *"How much do you charge for your inspections?"*

When it comes to determining home inspection fees, there are many variables that come into play in order to develop a home inspection fee schedule. It's important to know what to quote for an inspection before taking that first order.

Here are inspection variables that home inspectors consider when developing their inspection fee schedule: square footage, age, time-on-site, crawlspace, basement, foundation type, attached/detached garage, in-law quarters, out-buildings, pool, septic tank, part of the country, travel distance, price of house and/or knowing what the competition charges.

Here's how four inspectors might calculate their total inspection fee for a single family residence with a crawlspace, detached garage and located 35 miles away. The 1200sf house was built in 1954 with the local area home inspectors charging $275 to $450 for the inspection.

Inspector #1 – Not certified, licensed or insured…2 years experience
Inspector #2 – Certified or licensed, not insured …5 years experience
Inspector #3 – Certified or licensed, insured …5 years experience
Inspector #4 – Certified or licensed, insured…12 years experience

Inspector #1 – Charges $275 ($225 house + $25 age + $25 garage)
Inspector #2 – Charges $350 ($275 house + $25 garage + $50 crawlspace)
Inspector #3 – Charges $375 ($375 house + no additional fees for garage/crawlspace)
Inspector #4 – Charges $450 ($325 house + $25 age + $50 crawlspace + $25 garage + $25 mileage)

When a home buyer or real estate agent calls to schedule an inspection appointment, the pseudo conversation might go something like this:

Buyer: Hi, I'd like to schedule a home inspection
Office: Great. How many square feet is the house?
Buyer: 1200
Office: Our base fee is $325
Office: How old is the house?
Buyer: 65 years old
Office: There's an additional charge of $25 for older properties, as there's more time involved in preparing the report.
Office: Where's the property located?
Buyer: In Farawaytown.
Office: That's 35 miles away; we charge $25 for mileage.
Office: Does the house have a crawlspace?
Buyer: Yes it does.
Office: That's $50 to suit-up and inspect the crawlspace.

Office: You mentioned that there's a garage?
Buyer: Yes, but it's attached to the house.
Office: It's an extra $25 for the garage as we find more issues there.
Office: The total is $450, when would you like to schedule the inspection?

This approach calculates the total inspection fee during the phone conversation and tends to turn people off. Although this was **Inspector #4** with 12 years of experience, there's a chance they'll find another inspector.

When people call to schedule a home inspection, they want to know what you charge to come out, inspect the house and send a report. Most people assume there's one fee involved to do this.

Why **Inspector #3** is the better choice:

If you decide to have separate inspection fees that will be added to a base fee, calculate the fees in your head and quote the client a single dollar amount while you're on the phone. This is what **inspector #3** did, so that his $375 inspection fee includes inspecting everything on the property regardless of age, detached garage, crawl space and distance.

Paying for a home inspection should not be like buying a car with options. In the long run, inspection fees tend to average out. On Monday and Tuesday, you might inspection two old 1800sf Victorians with crawlspaces and detached garages 30 miles away; and on Wednesday and Thursday, you land a couple of 1500sf houses built within the past 5 years on slab foundations with attached garages in your town.

Savvy home buyers and realtors would have likely hired **inspector #3**. Most people who call an inspector don't know to ask if you're certified or licensed, whether or not you have E&O insurance, how much experience you have, and when can they expect the report.

Inspector #1 wasn't considered because the buyer discovered that he wasn't certified, licensed or insured and had only 2 years of experience. **Inspector #2** was certified or licensed, but not E&O insured though he had 5 years experience.

In determining your inspection fees, it's worth the time to find out what the competition charges. If you know a realtor, ask them what other home inspectors charge. There are also online inspection fee calculators that can be used.

If you charge too much, the client/agents may go with the competition. If you charge too little, you may not make a decent living. Experienced realtors shy away from 'cheap' inspection fees, knowing the inspector probably isn't getting many inspection requests and discounts his fees to entice people to use their service. There's a perceived association between quality of inspections and inspection fees. Charging too little may send the wrong message in that a lower inspection fee means a cheap or poor quality inspection.

When you're starting out, it's probably best to charge about what everyone else is charging in town. As your experience grows there will be a time to adjust the fees upward to reflect your expertise. There is no magic formula for calculating inspection fees. The best approach is to keep the inspection fee list simple by quoting one price that includes all the 'extras', and falls in the inspection fee range for your inspection area.

Another consideration is the amount of time it takes to inspect a property. The inspection time on a 60 year old, 1200 sq ft house can vary considerably between inspectors, depending on whether the house has been maintained or there is a lot of deferred maintenance and repairs. New inspectors may take 3-4 hours or longer, whereas an experienced inspector may complete the visual inspection in 1.5-2 hours. You should be sensitive to the home buyer's and agent's time. Most people don't like to stand around for hours waiting for the inspector to finish.

12

Please Sign Here

Inspection Agreement

THE TAG LINE: *"Don't leave home without it"* was developed in 1975 by David Ogilvy of Ogilvy & Mather advertising as part of one of his highly successful marketing ad campaigns. For the home inspector, the advice is: <u>don't go to an inspection without an inspection agreement in hand</u>. In other words, don't perform a home inspection without a signed home inspection contract before you start the inspection.

What is a home inspection agreement? It's an inspection contract that broadly includes:

- Scope of the inspection
- What's inspected
- What isn't inspected
- Inspection fee
- What happens if there's a complaint
- Signature, date and much more

Repeat after me, "*I will not conduct a home inspection without a signed inspection contract.*" It's one of the best things you can do to protect yourself in the event of a lawsuit. People sue people, and home inspectors should take steps to limit their liability during a home inspection.

Many state licensing boards and insurance companies require a signed inspection contract detailing what the inspection covers and what's not included. If you're a member of an inspection association like ASHI, CREIA, InterNACHI, NAHI and others, most can provide you with an inspection agreement.

Some inspectors create their own inspection contract. The business laws of the state in which your business is conducted need to be considered in order to write a good inspection contract. Consulting with a local, knowledgeable real estate attorney is recommended, if you're going it alone.

Ideally, before starting an inspection, it's to your legal advantage to have a signed inspection contract 48 hours before the scheduled inspection. Most states requiring home inspectors to be licensed require that the inspection agreement be signed in advance.

Today a digital (electronic) signature constitutes a binding signature. What is a digital signature? With the computer, it takes the concept of traditional paper-based signature and turns it into an electronic "fingerprint." This fingerprint, or coded message, is unique to both an inspection contract and the buyer/seller and binds both of them together.

There are online electronic signature companies such as Inspection Agreement and Inspection Support Network which allow you to upload your inspection agreement in advance of the scheduled home inspection, where the client can read it online and agree to the terms before you do the home inspection.

There will be times when the client doesn't own a computer to sign online in advance. You need to bring a two-part inspection agreement to the home inspection site, review and sign it with your client prior to conducting the home inspection. A copy of the inspection agreement should be included in the home inspection report.

13

Stepping On Stage

Are You Ready

You bought errors & omissions insurance, tools, equipment and software and set up an office. Hours were spent developing a comprehensive home inspection comment library. There were tag-along inspections, the neighbors' houses were inspected and practice reports generated.

Your business website is up and running and business cards have been dropped off at open houses and handed to everyone. Time has been spent in local real estate offices talking with agents and you've attended their weekly marketing meetings to introduce yourself. You joined the local chamber of commerce, and now your efforts have paid off.

Remember that super agent who recently called to schedule an inspection? The time has come to conduct your first, fee-paid home inspection. Make sure you have business cards and the tools/equipment you need. Bring a copy of the work order and the inspection agreement. Plan to arrive 15-20 minutes before the scheduled inspection start time.

When you arrive at the inspection site, the spotlight will be on you. It's like walking on stage to present three acts in a show:

Act I – **The Driveway Talk** sets the tone of the inspection with attendees.
Act II – **The Performance** is the inspection of the house, top to bottom.
Act III – **The Recap** summarizes inspection findings with clients and real estate agents and answers questions and concerns.

Act I, The Driveway Talk

Before the inspection begins, an important step for home inspectors is to set the tone of the inspection with the client, the person paying for the inspection, and to build a mini-relationship with them. People who know you are less likely to take you to court if a reportable condition was missed during the inspection. Verbal communication skills are very important when you are introduced to the client and their agent at the beginning of an inspection. Your challenge is to:

- Put people at ease
- Provide clear, concise explanations
- Act in a low-key, non-alarmist, matter of fact way
- Ensure verbal comments match report comments

It's about letting the client know what they can expect during the inspection and what will be inspected.

Home inspector: *"Good morning. How are you? How long have you been looking for a house (breaking the ice)?*

I'd like to take a few minutes to explain why you hired me and to review my inspection agreement. Usually there's money involved and your expectations are high, but nobody likes surprises. You don't want to move into the house and a week later discover there are problems that no one told you about.

My inspection starts with the roof and I work my way down the house, around the house, into the house, and if there's a crawlspace, I'll be going under the house. I also review the surrounding grading and drainage situations around the building. I look at everything that's readily accessible and visible.

There are two places in the house that I can't tell you anything about: I can't see inside of walls and I can't tell you about the condition of the main drain/waste pipe once it enters the dirt under the house.

You should know that I'm not going to find or point out everything that isn't perfect. I'm looking for big dollar repair items and serious health and safety concerns that may affect your decision to buy the house. In the course of my inspection I'll be noting all of the minor discrepancies that I encounter and taking photos to help identify conditions that need attention. The goal isn't to create a detailed repair list, but to help you understand the overall condition of the property"

"My job is to visually review the house, document observations, and make recommendations for further review but not to evaluate the performance of or disassemble appliances."

Inform the client, that your inspection is not a building code compliant inspection (city building inspectors), but rather a visual inspection to examine the condition of the building (home inspectors are generalists - they know a little about everything).

Respect the client and agent's time and set expectations on how long the inspection will last, *"It'll take approximately 1.5-3 hours to complete the inspection, depending on the condition of the house."*

By now the client should be feeling comfortable with you and it's the time to review the Inspection Agreement with the client and have it signed (if they haven't already signed online). Let the client know that they're welcome to accompany you during your inspection. Some home inspectors embrace this request, and others prefer to inspect alone without distraction.

If you want the client to tag along during the inspection process, say something like… *"You're welcome to join me as I inspect the property. However, for liability reasons, I won't be asking you to accompany me on the roof or in the attic and crawlspace. I encourage you to ask questions along the way."*

This author found out the hard way, that when a client accompanies the inspector, you're more apt to engage in conversation and miss reporting property conditions. An over-looked condition cost the author a couple of hundred dollars. Long explanations and constantly answering the client's questions puts an inspector at risk of over-looking conditions in need of repair; and dragging out the inspection time to the point that realtors will stop using you.

For those inspectors who want to inspect alone, you can say something like… *"You're welcome to tag along with me, but if you do, I can't hold a running conversation. I've found that when I start talking during my inspection, I miss things. I encourage you to go ahead of me and check out the house. Right now I don't know anything about the property, but when I'm finished with my inspection, you and I will walk around the property to discuss my findings. This will be the best time for you to ask any questions, because I've had a chance to learn about the condition of the house."*

This statement allows the inspector to focus on the job at hand. The thought here is that the inspector isn't distracted by questions and conversation and minimizes the chance of missing something during the inspection process. Upon hearing the above comment at least 97% of the author's clients say, *"No, no, I want you to look at everything"*

Act II – The Performance

Visually inspecting a house is the start of your performance - you're on stage. Being on stage can make some newbie inspectors a little nervous. Staying calm is in the preparation and training, as well as being a member of an inspection organization, taking home inspection classes, learning to write inspection reports, and practicing home inspections, all of which allow you to step on stage as a confident inspector.

Every home inspector develops their own approach to inspecting a house. Home inspectors can begin their inspection at the roof, while others may walk around the exterior of the house first. Some will always start at the front door and move clockwise around the house, others counter-clockwise. However you decide to inspect, follow the same methodology on every home that's inspected. This will provide consistency, minimize oversights, reduce inspection anxiety and build inspector confidence.

When experienced inspectors pull up in front of a house, they've already observed the condition of the sidewalk, driveway, walkway, lay of the land, roof type and whether or not they'll be walking on the roof. This is inspecting at the macro level (overall). As a new inspector, this should be your goal - to take in the big picture.

The time it takes to conduct an inspection is an important factor. A typical maintained 1200 sf. house takes a seasoned inspector between 1.5-2 hours to conduct the inspection. First time home inspectors should be a little more cautious and take additional time to ensure they've covered everything that can be visually observed. Following an inspection checklist ensures that a component of the house wasn't over-looked. Know that Realtors will not use your services if a 600sf condo takes 2 hours to inspect.

There should be two inspection conditions that inspectors have in back of their mind as they conduct their inspections: anything to do with water damage or leakage and conditions that can affect people's health and safety.

Water is considered one of the worst enemies of a house. Water intrusion and water leaks can do a lot of damage to a structure. The observant inspector is on the lookout for water stains, dripping faucets, paint bubbles, dry rot conditions, poor drainage around the house, water pipe leakage, bio-growth (mildew and mold), musty smells, gaps and cracks around sinks, bathtubs, showers, slow-draining fixtures, pipe corrosion, and the list goes on.

Looking for property conditions that affect people's health and safety should be an inspector's top priority during their inspection. This includes items such as exposed electrical wires, missing smoke detectors, tripping and falling hazards, walkway offsets, stair railings and guardrails, etc. Missing one of these conditions which causes a future injury, can find you talking in front of a judge.

Documenting and photographing during your inspection goes a long way to ensure that the inspection report accurately depicts the conditions of the property. Remember that there are several ways for inspectors to capture information about the house: a checklist report, paper and pen, camera, voice recorder, laptop, tablet, or smartphone.

Taking too many photos during the inspection can be a good thing, even though not all photos are used in the final report. There have been instances where inspectors have been challenged on what the conditions were on a property, and producing a photo from their archives saved the day. Typically, the number of photos taken during an inspection diminishes as inspection experience grows.

The key for a thorough inspection, regardless of your inspection style and experience, is to carry a detailed checklist of the house components to remind you what is inspected: roof, chimney, exterior, interior, kitchen, attic, bathroom, electrical, HVAC, plumbing, etc. Sometimes, the inspector gets caught up in the moment. For example, you see a foundation crack and focus on that, but fail to see a nearby cracked floor joist.

If you miss something during the inspection, it definitely makes you look unprofessional in the eyes of the home buyer and their agent when the condition is discovered later and you have to return to the inspection site. Failing to call out a condition on the property which requires attention (especially a big ticket repair item) can be damaging to your pocketbook and to your reputation. Your insurance company may also drop you.

When leaving the stage (you finished the inspection), cast doubt on yourself: Did I look at every accessible and visible part of this house? This is a really good time to pull out that detailed checklist and walk around the house a second time. There will be times when you say, *"I'm really glad I went back to look in the basement."*

Act III – Recap
Now that you've stepped off the stage, it's time to recap the inspection high points with the client. The focus should be on big ticket repairs, health and safety items, and anything related to water leakage and damage. Sometimes it's too much information for the client to include the deferred maintenance, minor repairs and/or recommended upgrades, as they feel overwhelmed with all the 'problems' especially with a first time home buyer. Focus on the meat and potatoes, not the cookie crumbs.

"...the bedroom door rubs its frame" vs. *"...the subfloor is damaged under the bathroom toilet"*

It's important to walk around the property with the client to talk about your findings to show them what they can expect in the report. This goes a long way in building that client-inspector relationship. It almost always eliminates phone calls from the buyer, as they've seen the conditions for themselves. While conducting your walk around, ask a client, if they have questions or concerns about the house conditions. It's another way for the inspector to put the client's mind at ease.

Most home buyers can be confused if you talk in an overly technical way with them. The average person doesn't know the trade names for most building components and conditions. Say that the water heater safety valve is leaking (point the valve out to the client) verses saying the water heater's temperature pressure relief valve is leaking.

Present your findings to the home buyer in an even tone of voice and follow the three D's format of your report comments – review Chapter 5: Describe, Disclose, Disclaim - when summarizing with the home buyer.

There's a vertical crack in the left side stemwall foundation. This is a common condition with poor drainage around the property. If there's water intrusion, it's possible to corrode the reinforcing steel inside the concrete foundation. A common repair is to seal the crack. We recommend review by an applicable licensed contractor who will evaluate and discuss the condition with you.

There have been home buyers who backed out of buying a house because the home inspector came on too aggressively and 'over-inflated' their comments to the buyer. When talking about big ticket items and/or health/safety concerns with the client; it should be in a low key, matter of fact tone. You don't want to develop a reputation as a "deal killer".

The phrase "deal killer" is used by some real estate agents to describe an inspector who gives home buyers unbiased information in an inspection report or communicates with the homebuyer in a highly charged manner *"...this foundation is shot and will cost you thousands of dollars to repair."* ... leading the buyer to back out of a deal in which the agent thought was a sure sale.

Simply put - a deal killer is an inspector making mountains out of molehills and doesn't know how to properly communicate with a buyer. Don't become known as a deal killer. Agents will drop you like a hot potato. Remember: The inspector's job is to provide the facts and conditions of a house in an unbiased manner.

Tip for home inspectors: Work on improving your communication skills. Be patient and thorough and answer questions in an understandable way. Listen and educate the home buyer/client about their home without boring, overwhelming or scaring them.

Getting Paid

To release the inspection report to the client, payment for your inspection time and pending report is collected by receiving cash, a check or credit card payment. There was a time when home inspectors accepted only cash or a check. Today, more people use credit cards for convenience and for less fuss when going to the bank ATM for cash or for carrying a check book. The ability to process credit cards is becoming more important for home inspectors to cater to home buying clients.

There are apps that can turn your smartphone or tablet into credit card accepting machines. Some popular credit card processing apps can be found at Pay Anywhere, Intuit GoPayment, or Square Register.

Also, home inspector business platforms like Inspection Support Network have payment systems where a home buyer/seller can pay for the inspection with a credit card online in advance of the home inspection or after the inspection. It is good business practice not to release an inspection report until payment has been received.

Your Report

The home inspection report is why the client hired you. A professional home inspection report lists the good along with the not-so-good. People will be better able to judge the state of the home if the report includes the areas needing attention as well as the positive points.

> (+) *"The half-bathroom toilet is a low water flow model for water conservation"*
>
> (-) *"There's water leakage under the kitchen sink at the left side water shutoff valve"*

Let the client know about the pending inspection report as to when they can expect to receive it and how they'll get the report. Whether you email the report, download it from the Internet, send it in the mail or hand-deliver it, it's important in today's real estate market to do this within 24 hours of the inspection, which has become the norm.

Be sure your report has been reviewed, edited and checked for grammar errors and typos. The inspection report is a reflection of you and your professionalism. Include a contact phone number in the report, so if the client has questions, they can call you.

When reports are well written and supported with photos, clients feel that they've received good valve for the home inspection and have a good understanding of the condition of the house they're contemplating buying or selling. Clients and real estate agents are more likely to refer you to others if they've received an informative and well written report, and know that you stand behind your work.

14

The Report

THE INSPECTION REPORT is where the rubber meets the road. The report represents the eyes, ears and experience of a home inspector. A solid report describes the condition of a house, what needs attention and makes recommendations as to what to do. Home inspection reports are the exclusive property of the person who paid the inspection fee. You should not discuss or distribute reports to others without a client's permission.

Field Notes

In the past, inspectors took field notes using pen and paper as they inspected a building and presented their findings verbally to home buyers.

This evolved to their field notes being typed up and delivered in the form of a written report. The inspection findings were documented, copied and distributed to all parties involved in the real estate transaction. Typed reports were and still are time-consuming.

Checklist

To speed up the onsite inspection and report process, checklist reports appeared where inspectors placed an X in a box next to a condition and sometimes wrote a short notation to further elaborate on a condition.

☒ SMOKE DETECTORS - *The hallway ceiling detector is hanging from its wires*

Putting an 'X' in a box is easier and faster than taking field notes and typing up a report. A drawback to the checklist report is the lack of detailed information or a brief explanation of what can happen if an inspection condition isn't addressed; and the absence of a recommendation for the client. This vagueness may come back to bite you if a client takes you to court.

Written

A written narrative report describes inspection conditions more clearly and follows the 3Ds (describe, disclose, disclaim) of an inspection comment.

No carbon monoxide (CO) detector was installed outside the bedroom area per requirements. This is a potential health and safety concern. CO alarms are required outside each sleeping area and on every level of the home, including basements. We recommend installing a CO detector outside the bedroom area prior to the close of the contingency period. CO detectors can plugged into an electrical wall outlet or installed on the wall or ceiling.

Editing the written inspection report ensures that your comments accurately describe the property. It's important to revise, edit and proofread the report before sending it to the client.

Proofreading means carefully reviewing your report to find and correct typographical errors and mistakes in grammar and spelling. Remember, the report is a reflection of you.

Inspection Programs

With the advent of the computer, software inspection programs were developed which combined the written narrative report and the checklist report. Inspection programs contain hundreds of basic inspection comments sorted into house categories: roof, electrical, windows, attic, etc.

These inspection programs allow inspectors to make observations out in the field and quickly select the appropriate comments using a laptop, a tablet or a smartphone, saving a lot of report writing and editing time back at the office.

Software inspection programs come with various inspection templates and a library of basic comments. The comments should be reviewed and edited/modified to ensure they meet the three Ds of a well-structured inspection comment: Describe, Disclosure, Disclaim. These inspection programs let you attach photos to comments. Photos have defended home inspectors who found themselves dragged into court.

Home inspection program companies to check out:

- Inspect IT
- 3D Inspection System
- Horizon by Carson Dunlop
- Home Inspector Pro
- HomeGauge
- Inspect Faster
- Inspect Express

15

Writing Right

Report Comments

THE HOME INSPECTION report is a collection of comments of an inspected property which represents the inspector's unbiased findings. Report comments are a reflection of a home inspector's education, professionalism, and attention to detail, the latter being an extremely important reflection.

Home buyers expect the home inspector to pay attention to the details of a building's condition and accurately describe those conditions in a report, which they're paying for.

Most home inspectors enjoy the inspection process and talk to their clients about what they observed during the inspection. What many inspectors don't realize is that they have to write a report, a report where the comments must be clear, concise and easy to read by the client.

It's very important to list in your report what you saw during the inspection and what you <u>didn't see</u> - "*Access to the attic cover was blocked by stored items in a closet and/or built-in closet shelving. We do not move personal possessions or disassemble shelving. We recommend removal of the stored items and/or shelving in order to conduct an inspection of the attic as there may be reportable conditions."*

Well-written report comments limit inspection liability. Use short, simple sentences and avoid difficult words. Write simple. Learn how to present your inspection findings in a non-threatening manner and in a way to limit lawsuits.

There's no room for poor writing skills, including improper grammar, wrong punctuation, spelling errors, incorrect sentence structure, and word choices.

Choose your words carefully. Saying, "the water heater is shot" can be substituted with a comment such as, "The water heater appears to be at the end of its service life."

Ensure that inspection comments address the three 'Ds':

<u>Describe</u> (identify) - What and where is the condition? What did you see?
Example: "There were exposed electrical wires in the utility room that weren't properly terminated."

<u>Disclose</u> (explain) – What does this mean? Is a person's health or safety affected?
Example: "We couldn't verify that these wires were not energized or have the possibility of becoming energized. This is a potential electrical shock concern."

<u>Disclaim</u> (recommendation) - What should be done? Who needs to be contacted?
Example: "We highly recommend review by a licensed electrician prior to the close of the contingency period."

Here's an example of an inspection comment following the 3Ds:

> "[describe] *There were exposed electrical wires in the utility room that weren't properly terminated.* [disclose] *We couldn't verify that these wires were not energized or have the possibility of becoming energized. This is a potential electrical shock concern.* [disclaim] *We highly recommend review by a licensed electrician prior to the close of the contingency period.*"

Inspection report writing classes can be found at local inspector chapter meetings, through your local or state inspection organization, at seminars, home inspection conferences, online, in books and on CDs. There are online discussions and chat rooms where other inspectors discuss topics, ask questions and mentor each other.

To avoid liability when writing inspection comments – Remember this: **Write what you see (and don't see)... Say what you write... Don't minimize anything.** It's the attention to detail, the thoroughness of your comments and how well your findings are communicated that will dictate the success or failure of your inspection company.

16

Super Service

Customer Service

WHAT IS CUSTOMER service? Customer service is how you deal with people before a home inspection, during the inspection and after the report has been sent. It's having an office, answering the phone by the 3rd ring, scheduling inspections, performing inspections, delivering reports, addressing clients' questions, dealing with complaints and above all, staying positive and being consistent.

Good customer service provides an experience that meets customer expectations. It produces satisfied clients and repeat business. Bad customer service usually generates complaints and can result in fewer inspections because home buyers and Realtors might take their business to another inspection company.

It's a fact that every home inspector sooner or later deals with a client's complaint. How an inspector receives and resolves a complaint is what makes or breaks a home inspection business. It took time, money and energy to market your company and for an agent or home buyer to schedule an inspection. Not responding to a complaint can lead to an agent never recommending your inspection services again or to a customer filing a lawsuit against your inspection company.

Missing a large foundation crack and not addressing the oversight with the client could cost $50,000 or more to repair. More likely, you'll be hearing from the client's attorney. Your insurance company may increase your premium or drop your insurance coverage altogether. If you elected not to purchase errors and omissions insurance, you could face bankruptcy.

It's wise to recognize that we're all human and mistakes happen. It's equally important to understand that most clients don't understand the scope of a home inspection. As an inspector, it's up to you to conduct the best inspection you can. Communicate the purpose of the inspection with your client and what they should expect, as well as how to deal with any and all complaints. It's also important to develop a philosophy on how you handle complaints. There is no right way to deal with complaints as each situation is different. It's about emotions and how the inspector chooses to communicate.

There are inspectors who take a stance of rigidly defending their report and not admitting there was an oversight.

Still, there are some who will acknowledge there's a problem, but direct their complaining client to a boilerplate disclaimer in the report or to a recommended follow-up review by a licensed contractor, and that they have no follow-up responsibility.

A professional home inspector acknowledges oversights, meets the client back at the inspection site to discuss the concern, and in the interest of goodwill, will pay for repairs and corrections that weren't identified in the inspection report.

In the home inspection business, when a client or agent has an issue or a complaint, it's because the inspection service is lacking in some manner. A complaint is an opportunity because it gives the home inspector a chance to improve their service. If the complaint or oversight is resolved to the client or agent's satisfaction, then all parties are happy because they know their issue was addressed. They will probably continue to use or recommend your inspection service or maybe not. It's so important to respond as soon as you can to any complaint.

A homebuyer moved into their house and discovered they had no hot water in the shower. They called their real estate agent to complain. The agent in turn contacted the home inspector he had recommended to find out why this wasn't mentioned in the inspection report. The inspector wound up paying for a plumber to make repairs. However, the agent never called that home inspector again. The agent felt embarrassed that he had referred the inspector and that the inspector made him look bad in the eyes of the homebuyer.

Some home inspection companies fail to realize just how important good customer service is for the overall health of their business. People will always remember if your customer service was really good or really bad. If you have good customer service, home buyers and real estate agents naturally assume you have a great inspection service. If you have bad customer service, people naturally assume your inspection service is poor and will call another inspector.

You should care a lot about the people associated with a home inspection since they are really the most important component of your business. Without clients, you won't have inspections. When you don't have inspections, you have no income, and without money, you can't pay your expenses. When you don't pay your expenses and bills, your business fails.

The positive note is that if your clients feel as though your company cares about them and provides outstanding customer service, then your clients and real estate agents will be much more likely to refer you to others, and that is how your business grows.

17

Within Reach

IF YOU'RE READING this, you're probably a motivated, hands-on individual who knows that becoming a home inspector can be a challenging, demanding and rewarding career.

You're comfortable knowing that hours upon hours of time will be spent researching inspection websites, joining an inspection association, attending training classes, developing a market plan, setting up an office, creating an inspection comment library, learning about report writing, marketing yourself, inspecting houses, and many other tasks. If you are passionate about what you do, want to build a successful career, have a desire to be the boss and put money in the bank, then being a home inspector is within your reach.

Do you have…
The drive to succeed, to experience everything a home inspection business has to offer, and to be the top inspector in your town?

The passion and motivation to know that something you're going to start will create a service for others, and that you're going to make it happen?

Do you want…

To be the boss, knowing you can do things better than the other inspection company, while understanding that taking the steps to become a home inspector will be on the one hand, motivating, and on the other hand, scary; but you'll be in control, because you're going to be the boss.

Yes, money is a motivating factor, but it should be at the bottom of your list. Do what you have a passion for and the money will follow.

Oh, by the Way…

There will be sunshine and rainy inspection days. Crawling on your belly in a tight and sometimes muddy crawlspace isn't exactly most people's view of a job they'd like to do. There will be times when the phone doesn't ring and times when you wish you were on vacation.

Traits to keep in mind for a successful career change:

- Focus on your goal of becoming a successful home inspector.
- Give it your all. Devote the time and effort to be successful.
- Know that many great things come from small beginnings.
- Think outside the box. What can you do that other inspectors don't?

- Accept failure. Look at obstacles as an opportunity to grow.
- Be an optimist. A career change takes time.

Remember, when someone asks you, as a home inspector, if a house can talk…and you answer, "*Yes it can,*" you've made a successful career change. It feels good to be a home inspector.

Standards of Practice

001 Roof

I. The inspector shall inspect from ground level or the eaves:
   A. the roof-covering materials;
   B. the gutters;
   C. the downspouts;
   D. the vents, flashing, skylights, chimney, and other roof penetrations; and
   E. the general structure of the roof from the readily accessible panels, doors or stairs.
II. The inspector shall describe:
   A. the type of roof-covering materials.
III. The inspector shall report as in need of correction:
   A. observed indications of active roof leaks.
III. The inspector is not required to:
   A. walk on any roof surface.
   B. predict the service life expectancy.
   C. inspect underground downspout diverter drainage pipes.
   D. remove snow, ice, debris or other conditions that prohibit the observation of the roof surfaces.
   E. move insulation.

F. inspect antennae, satellite dishes, lightning arresters, de-icing equipment, or similar attachments.
G. walk on any roof areas that appear, in the opinion of the inspector, to be unsafe.
H. walk on any roof areas if it might, in the opinion of the inspector, cause damage.
I. perform a water test.
J. warrant or certify the roof.
K. confirm proper fastening or installation of any roof-covering material.

002 Exterior

I. The inspector shall inspect:
   A. the exterior wall-covering materials, flashing and trim;
   B. all exterior doors;
   C. adjacent walkways and driveways;
   D. stairs, steps, stoops, stairways and ramps;
   E. porches, patios, decks, balconies and carports;
   F. railings, guards and handrails;
   G. the eaves, soffits and fascia;
   H. a representative number of windows; and
   I. vegetation, surface drainage, retaining walls and grading of the property, where they may adversely affect the structure due to moisture intrusion.
II. The inspector shall describe:
   A. the type of exterior wall-covering materials.
III. The inspector shall report as in need of correction:
   A. any improper spacing between intermediate balusters, spindles and rails.

IV. The inspector is not required to:
   A. inspect or operate screens, storm windows, shutters, awnings, fences, outbuildings, or exterior accent lighting.
   B. inspect items that are not visible or readily accessible from the ground, including window and door flashing.
   C. inspect or identify geological, geotechnical, hydrological or soil conditions.
   D. inspect recreational facilities or playground equipment.
   E. inspect seawalls, break-walls or docks.
   F. inspect erosion-control or earth-stabilization measures.
   G. inspect for safety-type glass.
   H. inspect underground utilities.
   I. inspect underground items.
   J. inspect wells or springs.
   K. inspect solar, wind or geothermal systems.
   L. inspect swimming pools or spas.
   M. inspect wastewater treatment systems, septic systems or cesspools.
   N. inspect irrigation or sprinkler systems.
   O. inspect drainfields or dry wells.
   P. determine the integrity of multiple-pane window glazing or thermal window seals.

003 Basement, Foundation, Crawlspace & Structure

I. The inspector shall inspect:
   A. the foundation;
   B. the basement;
   C. the crawlspace; and

D. structural components.
II. The inspector shall describe:
   A. the type of foundation; and
   B. the location of the access to the under-floor space.
III. The inspector shall report as in need of correction:
   A. observed indications of wood in contact with or near soil;
   B. observed indications of active water penetration;
   C. observed indications of possible foundation movement, such as sheetrock cracks, brick cracks, out-of-square door frames, and unlevel floors; and
   D. any observed cutting, notching and boring of framing members that may, in the inspector's opinion, present a structural or safety concern.
IV. The inspector is not required to:
   A. enter any crawlspace that is not readily accessible, or where entry could cause damage or pose a hazard to the inspector.
   B. move stored items or debris.
   C. operate sump pumps with inaccessible floats.
   D. identify the size, spacing, span or location or determine the adequacy of foundation bolting, bracing, joists, joist spans or support systems.
   E. provide any engineering or architectural service.
   F. report on the adequacy of any structural system or component.

004 Heating

I. The inspector shall inspect:
   A. the heating system, using normal operating controls.

II. The inspector shall describe:
   A. the location of the thermostat for the heating system;
   B. the energy source; and
   C. the heating method.
III. The inspector shall report as in need of correction:
   A. any heating system that did not operate; and
   B. if the heating system was deemed inaccessible.
IV. The inspector is not required to:
   A. inspect or evaluate the interior of flues or chimneys, fire chambers, heat exchangers, combustion air systems, fresh-air intakes, humidifiers, dehumidifiers, electronic air filters, geothermal systems, or solar heating systems.
   B. inspect fuel tanks or underground or concealed fuel supply systems.
   C. determine the uniformity, temperature, flow, balance, distribution, size, capacity, BTU, or supply adequacy of the heating system.
   D. light or ignite pilot flames.
   E. activate heating, heat pump systems, or other heating systems when ambient temperatures or other circumstances are not conducive to safe operation or may damage the equipment.
   F. override electronic thermostats.
   G. evaluate fuel quality.
   H. verify thermostat calibration, heat anticipation, or automatic setbacks, timers, programs or clocks.

005 Cooling

I. The inspector shall inspect:
   A. the cooling system using normal operating controls.
II. The inspector shall describe:
   A. the location of the thermostat for the cooling system; and
   B. the cooling method.
III. The inspector shall report as in need of correction:
   A. any cooling system that did not operate; and
   B. if the cooling system was deemed inaccessible.
IV. The inspector is not required to:
   A. determine the uniformity, temperature, flow, balance, distribution, size, capacity, BTU, or supply adequacy of the cooling system.
   B. inspect portable window units, through-wall units, or electronic air filters.
   C. operate equipment or systems if the exterior temperature is below 65° Fahrenheit, or when other circumstances are not conducive to safe operation or may damage the equipment.
   D. inspect or determine thermostat calibration, cooling anticipation, or automatic setbacks or clocks.
   E. examine electrical current, coolant fluids or gases, or coolant leakage.

006 Plumbing

I. The inspector shall inspect:
   A. the main water supply shut-off valve;

B. the main fuel supply shut-off valve;
C. the water heating equipment, including the energy source, venting connections, temperature/pressure-relief (TPR) valves, Watts 210 valves, and seismic bracing;
D. interior water supply, including all fixtures and faucets, by running the water;
E. all toilets for proper operation by flushing;
F. all sinks, tubs and showers for functional drainage;
G. the drain, waste and vent system; and
H. drainage sump pumps with accessible floats.

II. The inspector shall describe:
A. whether the water supply is public or private based upon observed evidence;
B. the location of the main water supply shut-off valve;
C. the location of the main fuel supply shut-off valve;
D. the location of any observed fuel-storage system; and
E. the capacity of the water heating equipment, if labeled.

III. The inspector shall report as in need of correction:
A. deficiencies in the water supply by viewing the functional flow in two fixtures operated simultaneously;
B. deficiencies in the installation of hot and cold water faucets;
C. mechanical drain stops that were missing or did not operate if installed in sinks, lavatories and tubs; and
D. toilets that were damaged, had loose connections to the floor, were leaking, or had tank components that did not operate.

IV. The inspector is not required to:
A. light or ignite pilot flames.
B. measure the capacity, temperature, age, life expectancy or adequacy of the water heater.

C. inspect the interior of flues or chimneys, combustion air systems, water softener or filtering systems, well pumps or tanks, safety or shut-off valves, floor drains, lawn sprinkler systems, or fire sprinkler systems.
D. determine the exact flow rate, volume, pressure, temperature or adequacy of the water supply.
E. determine the water quality, potability or reliability of the water supply or source.
F. open sealed plumbing access panels.
G. inspect clothes washing machines or their connections.
H. operate any valve.
I. test shower pans, tub and shower surrounds or enclosures for leakage or functional overflow protection.
J. evaluate the compliance with conservation, energy or building standards, or the proper design or sizing of any water, waste or venting components, fixtures or piping.
K. determine the effectiveness of anti-siphon, back-flow prevention or drain-stop devices.
L. determine whether there are sufficient cleanouts for effective cleaning of drains.
M. evaluate fuel storage tanks or supply systems.
N. inspect wastewater treatment systems.
O. inspect water treatment systems or water filters.
P. inspect water storage tanks, pressure pumps, or bladder tanks.
Q. evaluate wait time to obtain hot water at fixtures, or perform testing of any kind to water heater elements.
R. evaluate or determine the adequacy of combustion air.

S. test, operate, open or close: safety controls, manual stop valves, temperature/pressure-relief valves, control valves, or check valves.
T. examine ancillary or auxiliary systems or components, such as, but not limited to, those related to solar water heating and hot water circulation.
U. determine the existence or condition of polybutylene plumbing.

007 Electrical

I. The inspector shall inspect:
A. the service drop;
B. the overhead service conductors and attachment point;
C. the service head, gooseneck and drip loops;
D. the service mast, service conduit and raceway;
E. the electric meter and base;
F. service-entrance conductors;
G. the main service disconnect;
H. panelboards and over-current protection devices (circuit breakers and fuses);
I. service grounding and bonding;
J. a representative number of switches, lighting fixtures and receptacles, including receptacles observed and deemed to be arc-fault circuit interrupter (AFCI)-protected using the AFCI test button, where possible;
K. all ground-fault circuit interrupter receptacles and circuit breakers observed and deemed to be GFCIs using a GFCI tester, where possible; and
L. smoke and carbon-monoxide detectors.

II. The inspector shall describe:
   A. the main service disconnect's amperage rating, if labeled; and
   B. the type of wiring observed.
III. The inspector shall report as in need of correction:
   A. deficiencies in the integrity of the service-entrance conductors' insulation, drip loop, and vertical clearances from grade and roofs;
   B. any unused circuit-breaker panel opening that was not filled;
   C. the presence of solid conductor aluminum branch-circuit wiring, if readily visible;
   D. any tested receptacle in which power was not present, polarity was incorrect, the cover was not in place, the GFCI devices were not properly installed or did not operate properly, evidence of arcing or excessive heat, and where the receptacle was not grounded or was not secured to the wall; and
   E. the absence of smoke detectors.
IV. The inspector is not required to:
   A. insert any tool, probe or device into the main panelboard, sub-panels, distribution panelboards, or electrical fixtures.
   B. operate electrical systems that are shut down.
   C. remove panelboard cabinet covers or dead fronts.
   D. operate or re-set over-current protection devices or overload devices.
   E. operate smoke or carbon-monoxide detectors.
   F. measure or determine the amperage or voltage of the main service equipment, if not visibly labeled.
   G. inspect the fire and alarm system or components.

H. inspect the ancillary wiring or remote-control devices.
I. activate any electrical systems or branch circuits that are not energized.
J. inspect low-voltage systems, electrical de-icing tapes, swimming pool wiring, or any time-controlled devices.
K. verify the service ground.
L. inspect private or emergency electrical supply sources, including, but not limited to: generators, windmills, photovoltaic solar collectors, or battery or electrical storage facility.
M. inspect spark or lightning arrestors.
N. inspect or test de-icing equipment.
O. conduct voltage-drop calculations.
P. determine the accuracy of labeling.
Q. inspect exterior lighting.

008 Fireplace

I. The inspector shall inspect:
   A. readily accessible and visible portions of the fireplaces and chimneys;
   B. lintels above the fireplace openings;
   C. damper doors by opening and closing them, if readily accessible and manually operable; and
   D. cleanout doors and frames.
II. The inspector shall describe:
   A. the type of fireplace.
III. The inspector shall report as in need of correction:
   A. evidence of joint separation, damage or deterioration of the hearth, hearth extension or chambers;

B. manually operated dampers that did not open and close;
C. the lack of a smoke detector in the same room as the fireplace;
D. the lack of a carbon-monoxide detector in the same room as the fireplace; and
E. cleanouts not made of metal, pre-cast cement, or other non-combustible material.

IV. The inspector is not required to:
A. inspect the flue or vent system.
B. inspect the interior of chimneys or flues, fire doors or screens, seals or gaskets, or mantels.
C. determine the need for a chimney sweep.
D. operate gas fireplace inserts.
E. light pilot flames.
F. determine the appropriateness of any installation.
G. inspect automatic fuel-fed devices.
H. inspect combustion and/or make-up air devices.
I. inspect heat-distribution assists, whether gravity-controlled or fan-assisted.
J. ignite or extinguish fires.
K. determine the adequacy of drafts or draft characteristics.
L. move fireplace inserts, stoves or firebox contents.
M. perform a smoke test.
N. dismantle or remove any component.
O. perform a National Fire Protection Association (NFPA)-style inspection.
P. perform a Phase I fireplace and chimney inspection.

009 Attic, Insulation & Ventilation

I. The inspector shall inspect:
   A. insulation in unfinished spaces, including attics, crawlspaces and foundation areas;
   B. ventilation of unfinished spaces, including attics, crawlspaces and foundation areas; and
   C. mechanical exhaust systems in the kitchen, bathrooms and laundry area.
II. The inspector shall describe:
   A. the type of insulation observed; and
   B. the approximate average depth of insulation observed at the unfinished attic floor area or roof structure.
III. The inspector shall report as in need of correction:
   A. the general absence of insulation or ventilation in unfinished spaces.
IV. The inspector is not required to:
   A. enter the attic or any unfinished spaces that are not readily accessible, or where entry could cause damage or, in the inspector's opinion, pose a safety hazard.
   B. move, touch or disturb insulation.
   C. move, touch or disturb vapor retarders.
   D. break or otherwise damage the surface finish or weather seal on or around access panels or covers.
   E. identify the composition or R-value of insulation material.
   F. activate thermostatically operated fans.
   G. determine the types of materials used in insulation or wrapping of pipes, ducts, jackets, boilers or wiring.
   H. determine the adequacy of ventilation.

010 Doors, Windows & Interior

I. The inspector shall inspect:
    A. a representative number of doors and windows by opening and closing them;
    B. floors, walls and ceilings;
    C. stairs, steps, landings, stairways and ramps;
    D. railings, guards and handrails; and
    E. garage vehicle doors and the operation of garage vehicle door openers, using normal operating controls.
II. The inspector shall describe:
    A. a garage vehicle door as manually-operated or installed with a garage door opener.
III. The inspector shall report as in need of correction:
    A. improper spacing between intermediate balusters, spindles and rails for steps, stairways, guards and railings;
    B. photo-electric safety sensors that did not operate properly; and
    C. any window that was obviously fogged or displayed other evidence of broken seals.
IV. The inspector is not required to:
    A. inspect paint, wallpaper, window treatments or finish treatments.
    B. inspect floor coverings or carpeting.
    C. inspect central vacuum systems.
    D. inspect for safety glazing.
    E. inspect security systems or components.
    F. evaluate the fastening of islands, countertops, cabinets, sink tops or fixtures.

G. move furniture, stored items, or any coverings, such as carpets or rugs, in order to inspect the concealed floor structure.
H. move suspended-ceiling tiles.
I. inspect or move any household appliances.
J. inspect or operate equipment housed in the garage, except as otherwise noted.
K. verify or certify the proper operation of any pressure-activated auto-reverse or related safety feature of a garage door.
L. operate or evaluate any security bar release and opening mechanisms, whether interior or exterior, including their compliance with local, state or federal standards.
M. operate any system, appliance or component that requires the use of special keys, codes, combinations or devices.
N. operate or evaluate self-cleaning oven cycles, tilt guards/latches, or signal lights.
O. inspect microwave ovens or test leakage from microwave ovens.
P. operate or examine any sauna, steam-generating equipment, kiln, toaster, ice maker, coffee maker, can opener, bread warmer, blender, instant hot-water dispenser, or other small, ancillary appliances or devices.
Q. inspect elevators.
R. inspect remote controls.
S. inspect appliances.
T. inspect items not permanently installed.
U. discover firewall compromises.
V. inspect pools, spas or fountains.

W. determine the adequacy of whirlpool or spa jets, water force, or bubble effects.
X. determine the structural integrity or leakage of pools or spas.

Code of Ethics for Home Inspectors

I. **Duty to the Public**
   1. The inspector shall abide by the Code of Ethics and substantially follow their organization's Standards of Practice.
   2. The inspector shall not engage in any practices that could be damaging to the public or bring discredit to the home inspection industry.
   3. The inspector shall be fair, honest, impartial, and act in good faith in dealing with the public.
   4. The inspector shall not discriminate in any business activities on the basis of race, color, religion, sex, national origin, familial status, sexual orientation, or handicap, and shall comply with all federal, state and local laws concerning discrimination.
   5. The inspector shall be truthful regarding his/her services and qualifications.
   6. The inspector shall not:
      a. have any disclosed or undisclosed conflict of interest with the client;
      b. accept or offer any disclosed or undisclosed commissions, rebates, profits, or other benefit from real

estate agents, brokers, or any third parties having financial interest in the sale of the property;
   c. or offer or provide any disclosed or undisclosed financial compensation directly or indirectly to any real estate agent, real estate broker, or real estate company for referrals or for inclusion on lists of preferred and/or affiliated inspectors or inspection companies.
7. The inspector shall not release any information about the inspection or the client to a third party unless doing so is necessary to protect the safety of others, to comply with a law or statute, or both of the following conditions are met:
   a. the client has been made explicitly aware of what information will be released, to whom, and for what purpose, and;
   b. the client has provided explicit, prior written consent for the release of his/her information.
8. The inspector shall always act in the interests of the client unless doing so violates a law, statute, or their Code of Ethics.
9. The inspector shall use a written contract that specifies the services to be performed, limitations of services, and fees.
10. The inspector shall comply with all government rules and licensing requirements of the jurisdiction where s/he conducts business.
11. The inspector shall not perform or offer to perform, for an additional fee, any repairs or associated services to

the structure for which the member or member's company has prepared a home inspection report for a period of 12 months. This provision shall not include services to components and/or systems that are not included in their organization's Standards of Practice.

II. Duty to Continue Education
1. The inspector shall comply with their organization's current continuing education requirements.
2. The inspector shall pass their organization's inspection exam.

III. Duty to the Home Inspection Profession
1. The inspector shall strive to improve the home inspection industry by sharing his/her lessons and/or experiences for the benefit of all. This does not preclude the member from copyrighting or marketing his/her expertise to other Inspectors or the public in any manner permitted by law.
2. The inspector shall assist their organization's leadership in disseminating and publicizing the benefits of their membership.
3. The inspector shall not engage in any act or practice that could be deemed damaging, seditious or destructive to their organization, fellow organization members, organization employees, leadership or director.
4. The inspector shall abide by their organization's current membership requirements.
5. The inspector shall abide by their organization's current message board rules.

Made in the USA
Lexington, KY
31 May 2019